Bring a Torch, Jeannette, Is

Fr. Horn

arranged by Luther Henderson

Ding Dong! Merrily On High

Fr. Horn

traditional carol
arranged by Luther Henderson

(Play in absence of chimes-in buckets or into stand.)

Go Tell It On The Mountain

Fr. Horn

19th century Negro Spiritual
arranged by Luther Henderson

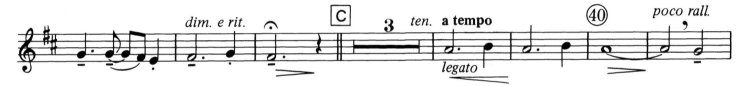

God Rest Ye Merry Gentlemen

Fr. Horn

traditional London carol, 19th century tune
arranged by Luther Henderson

Here We Come A-Wassailing

Fr. Horn

traditional carol from the north of England
arranged by Luther Henderson

The Huron Carol

traditional carol
arranged by Luther Henderson

Fr. Horn

I Saw Three Ships

Fr. Horn

traditional English carol
arranged by Luther Henderson

Sussex Carol

Fr. Horn

traditional English carol
arranged by Luther Henderson

Introduction